THE CHOSEN COLOR
pretty dark

BRE ASHLEY

the chosen color.pretty dark
copyright © 2021 bre ashley

FIRST PRINTED IN 2021 ISBN 979-8-52-089652-4

all rights reserved. no part of this publication may be reproduced, distributed, or transmitted in any form or by any means, including photocopying, recording, or other electronic or mechanical methods, without the prior written permission of the publisher, except in the case of brief quotations embodied in critical reviews and certain other noncommercial uses permitted by copyright law. For permission requests, contact BA publishing.

events in the book are the author's memories from her perspective. parts of this book is are fictional perspectives guided by real events. certain names have been changed or omitted to protect the identities of those involved as needed. this material is not to be used as legal or medical advice.

graphic designer: bre ashley
editor: ba publishing
vector graphics: www.canva.com
photography: IG @catharperphotography
makeup: IG @beat.by.burst

LIVE YOUR DREAMS   LOVE YOUR STORY
www.bapublishingco.com

Contact Information

www.jetblacktheprelude.com

IG: @jetblacktheprelude

breashley@jetblacktheprelude.com

other books by the author

"24 hours to a New U"

JET BLACK: the prelude Volume 1

pretty dark

BRE ASHLEY

DEDICATION

the color of you
the color of me
the color of us
the color we only see
when we close our eyes
to my sister, the chosen one
the mirror of my younger self

CONTENTS

part 1 (In the dark)	1
what is darkness?	2
(part 1)	2
conversations	4
(in the dark)	4
more glory	7
s.o.u.l	10
part 2 (solitary)	12
Reform me	14
behind the bars	20
Just like George	24
(1969)	24
plaintiff prayer	30
No standing	34

Executive Poet	45
Guilty	47
stalemate	52
solitary (freestyle)	54
doj	57
(don't oppress the jamz)	57
Soul motion	59
(her ocean)	59
part 3 (four roses)	61
if i die	63
aopolo"G"	68
the Sentence	74
cookies n' cream	77
always hungry	80
appetite changes	83

c.b.d.	86
hydrate	88
if i'm being played	89
(ode to dmx)	89
No more i.c.e	93
Four roses	98
part 4 (memory foam)	100
after dark	102
Dear bourbon pt. 1	106
The ryde	109
r.u.f.f	111
bulleits	114
my mind, my song	116
Black b.i.r.d	121
altitude	126

poe-tree	134
the color of forever	137
In this room	141
Memory foam	143
my mattress is Black	145
Lover's block	149
part 5 (tomorrow's sorrow)	151
w.a.l.k.	154
my Back	155
Black vessels	159
Here & Now	161
Psoas games	165
Sensations	167
Candlelight in me	169
part 6 (pretty girl gambit)	179

pretty dark	180
Don't	183
Pretty girl gambit	186
v.i.p	190
c.c. clout	192
Still sittin' pretty	195
Innocent curls	198
p.g.p	200
November remembers (part 1)	201 201
Princess of peace	204
birth marks	207
november Remembers ((part 2)	210 210
what is darkness?	211

(part 2)	211
What Did You Think of pretty dark?	212
Author's Note	215
About the author	216

"i lost myself,
thats why I had to go,
then the light came up,
right after i forgave me,
i prayed so hard,
i thought i'd lose my mind...

do you know things get better, do you know, i had to grow the rose in the dark, but im a little stronger baby, a little wiser baby"

— cleo soul

part 1 (In the dark)

WHAT IS DARKNESS?
(part 1)

what is darkness?
    is it a place
        on a map
            in humanities'
                habitat

what is darkness?
    have i been there before?
        does it smell like this?
            like mahogany
                like jazz
                    cloves

how long was i there?

    was i alone?

        could i see?

            was i alone?

                could i see?

CONVERSATIONS
(in the dark)

luke wasn't warm

the bible wasn't hot

when I get cold,

the pen gets hot

flames from the pain

flow from the the

front lobe of my brain

the kaos in my veins

calmed by the iv

injected vices

fluid was my soul

cold was my heart

my inner t.h.u.g.

tough

heart

unconditional

gangsta

conversations in the dark with a tough heart, unconditional gangsta love sent from above

conversations in the dark
helped me find my light

i can still hear the music in my bones
and poems in my soul

i can still hear the MUSIC in my bones and poems in my soul

MORE GLORY

give me more

give me more

more pain

more agony

more misery

more pain

Jesus could take more

Jesus could take more

give me more

give me more

more pain

more joy

more glory

oh lord

more pain

more joy

more glory

oh lord

Jesus took more

Jesus took more

give me more pain

give me more glory

give me more words

to write my story

more PAIN
more glory

S.O.U.L

no words
to title my lifeblood,
leaking from my s.o.u.l.
song lyrics exit
pierced wounds
by evading bone graft
and sutures.

only he knows the melody
as we patiently await vocals and keys
to sing over you, poetically
with my steadfast, oiled
unconditional love
[s.o.u.l.]

i gave u my

S.O.U.L

steadfast.

oiled.

unconditional.

love.

part 2 (solitary)

"CAN YOU STAND IN MY PLACE, GOT ANXIETY"

- FOUSHEE

REFORM ME

i keep on writin'
with no pens
traded vodka for gin

bombay blues
i keep on drinkin'
words, neat
ice, never melts

in an out, i fall
martini spills it all

i keep on trying
these thoughts never fail
no new friends
no funds for bail
REFORM ME

"CAN I TRY ON YOUR LIFE,
WANNA STAY FOR A
WHILE...
CAN I BORROW YOUR TIME
MACHINE"

- FOUSHEE

i keep on writing
in solitude
with attitude
anti-social
media isn't worthy
of my tea
splenda, tainted
a life of lemons
intertwined rose hibiscus

i keep on flowing
growing
glowing
with a smooth, healthy
green tea groove
cast iron approved

"I ADMIT, I CAN'T LIVE
WHEN I THINK TOO MUCH,
TOO MUCH ON MY MIND"

- LIL WAYNE

BEHIND THE BARS

i'm locked up

[my pen is the key]

i'm locked up

[my pen is the key]

[behind the bars]

quarantined reform

too much vitamin [C]

immunity, orange suit

transfers

[behind the bars]
arrested respirations
of the innocent youth
send them a [jet]
fly it with truth

i'm locked up
[MY PEN IS THE KEY]
i'm locked up
[MY PEN IS THE KEY]

[behind the bars]
my repertoire flows

[jet] black [bar] codes
my mind is sold

price is tenfold
this world is so cold
lovely melodies
overpriced scars
persecuted thoughts*
bars sing to me

*if u find me behind the bars, leave
this book on the ground, with my pen, i
am found

"FREE FROM HOW THEY
SEE US
FREEDOM, WON'T YOU
FREE US?"

- H.E.R.

JUST LIKE GEORGE
(1969)

my uncle said.....

"ONLY FREE APPROXIMATELY"

- BLACK THOUGHT

they hate us when were good,
they hate us when we're bad

"LOOK AT THIS AMERICAN HISTORY OF THUGGERY"

- BLACK THOUGHT

i would have been dead just like
george but my mama was there...

"I HAD TO WALK OUT WITH
MY ARMS UP...AINT TOO BIG
TO PRAY LAST MINUTE"

- BRENT FAIYAZ

PLAINTIFF PRAYER

jah

grant me justice

in this case so

I can build a career

based on faith

1 litigant

1 love

1 law

"JUST KEEP ON BEING THE VOICE, I BE THE HERO"

- LIL BABY/LIL DURK

1 litigant
1 law
1 love

"AM I CIVILIZED, WHY I GOTTA PROVE THAT?"

- BLACK THOUGHT

NO STANDING

no standing
[in the way] of BRE
in the way of my dreams

paid my debt with injuries w/ my own
grand jury
indicted myself,
3 counts of mental health

"EVERYTHING I WORKED FOR, I GOTTA LOSE THAT?"

- BLACK THOUGHT

casual connection is black
like my history, redressability
dressed the law in pink
made my con law book think

w/ saltwater pearls on each page rbg
dissents NFIB
pages, we highlight
outlines, made in the twilight
zone of my life

express or implied
i'm executing my powers
preemptive rights
to my Tubman dollars

u have no standing
judge, remand him
in the interest of justice
he admitted his negligence
when second semester began
check the brief he highlights
in the zone of twilight
traded his fees for a guilty plea

for misrepresenting BRE
charm was not free
my drop top v. attorney #3

3 corners A B C
fraud triangle cuts deep
even Covid-19
can smell a ponzi scheme
don't violate the UCC

queen of compliance
princess of torts
power and passion

aaliyah taught me how to

rock the boat,

eliminate the middle

judge called me a lit-igator
then refused to order the lizard

SMH

pay now, not later

which side will you stand?

"TIPPING ON A TIGHTROPE AND I DON'T LIKE HEIGHTS"

- BLACK THOUGHT

double vision, double digits
this concussion

no standing in the way of BRE
in the way of my dreams
casual connection is black
like my history, redressability
dressed the law in pink
made my con law book think

"AND I'M SPEAKING THE TRUTH, REGARDLESS OF WHAT YOU'VE BEEN TEACHING THE YOUTH"

- BLACK THOUGHT

Jah's loves is supreme
law of the land
taught me everything
about man

Apple not yet ripe
Armed Strife in Eden
Gave me horsepower
No pony
Jah will repay me
A lamb in my lemon
ugg shoes now
A lion king came thru
When I had nothing left
But the gift of poetry
standing judiciously

"I'M GONNA HURT YOU FIRST,

- Niia

EXECUTIVE POET

enumerated [black girl]
article 1 section 8
Power of of the plate
Civil cups she fills up
then wash away yesterday

enumerated [black girl]
Defend the troops
Of your faith and
ur truth

enumerated [black girl]
Vested in the light
[darkside] confers hues
Executive power in you

Nina authorized blues
H.e.r approved the prelude
With an executive order
For holding onto you
poetry privilege

24 hour verdict
jurors debate
her romantic fate
guilty after one date

1 juror dismissed
they shared 1 kiss
same lips
evidence in her hips

"I'LL BE THE ONE WHO MAKES YOU CRY"

— Niia

closing argument
attorney grace
the real AG
would never let me plea
with my heart on my sleeve

guilty hearts matter
tattooed on his knee
cross examine the ink
til it bleeds pink
legal reverie

"I'LL BE THE ONE WHO GETS TO DECIDE"

- NIIA

"WORE A BLACK DRESS
JUST TO LET YOU DOWN
ONE MORE TIME"

- NIIA

STALEMATE

pain is a game
no one wins
in the path it moves
yet we continue to play
stalemate with you
black king
go forward
black queen
move backward
pain is a game
no one wins
yet I continue to play
stalemate with you

"ADDICTED TO THE PAIN,
IF I WAS YOU I'D RUN"

- Niia

SOLITARY (freestyle)

Queen of hearts
no king
black diamonds
no ring

black bars
deck of cards
this game left me scars

solitary
i need Mary!
no more drama

Mary, my Queen of hearts
my mama since 86
breastmilk was lit
i had rhymes in the womb
i started reading too soon

at four i had a revelation
at thirty-four, a consecration

Queen of hearts
no king
black diamonds
no ring

solitary confinement
my lineage alignment

"BLACK AS THE JUDGE ROBE WHEN THE CASE CLOSED, NOW YOUR LIFE ON THE BACK BURNER"

- D SMOKE

(don't oppress the jamz)

The first time I heard d smoke
My ears choked from theee smoke

I was behind bars
Had to submit an appeal
For the scars

Apple said my sound was too loud
I updated my software the music was found

It's just a black habit
To have my hair black
And my music loud

Gotta pay attention to the bass in this case
...the treble in the charges

The frequency of the convicted behind bars

Let's listen

SOUL MOTION
(her ocean)

she loves in soul motion
he rides the waves of her ocean

then she's in too deep
do black mermaids weep?

when the tide gets too high
there can be no goodbye

she loves in soul motion
one kiss...one date
determines their fate
two souls, one motion

focus on her

focus on me

dive into me
dive into my ocean

before you free me

part 3 (four roses)

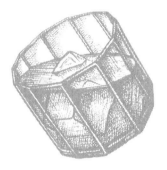

"I FIND TIME'S NEVER A FRIEND BUT LIKE FINE WINE, A LIFETIME SWEETENS THE BLEND"

— NIIA

IF I DIE

nails in my spine
metal in my heart
my pulse, too high

am i being crucified?
[CRUCIFIED]
for a name i held high?
[SO HIGH]

where will i go if i die?
[IF I DIE]
is my legacy alive?
[ALIVE]

i feel
i feel like
i feel like
i'm on the cross
i feel like i'm on the cross,

paying the costs

like a slave that's lost

like a slave that's loss,

too much blood

when she cut across

when they cut across

so many scars,
so many scars
when they cut across

nails deep in my spine
this pain is so alive
treble in my soul
my meters in my pulse
poems of my heart

am i being crucified?
for a name i held high?

where will i go if i die?
[IF I DIE]
is my legacy alive?
[ALIVE]

i'd rather die
with my name
held HIGH,

than let
my pride
be sanctified
by pain ALIVE.

"I'M GOOD FOR THE EGO
BUT BAD FOR THE SOUL"

- Niia

APOLO"G"

only date real G's

the gangstas that know how to make apologies

i love it when they look into these light brown eyes and say sorry

i love it when they make my kush mascara bleed

lashes so soft from the apologies

only date real G's
the gangstas that know
how to make apologies

SORRY,
i sold my nikes
tired of stepping on our love

SORRY,
i trashed the jewelry box
my apologies, first love

SORRY,
i blocked u
but u blocked my dream

SORRY,

i hated flowers

only accept

black diamonds

maybe black roses

my apologies come in small doses

filled with art

SORRY,

i'm pretty dark

SORRY,

for the vibes

SORRY,

for the love u felt inside

SORRY,

my heart hides

Sorry,

i'm pretty

so pretty in the dark

I HOPE YOU ACCEPT THIS POETRY

"I DON'T MAKE MISTAKES,
TALLY UP MY L'S AND
THEY CORRELATE"

- FOUSHEE

"CAUSE RIGHT NOW, WHAT I HAVE TO DO IS, I GOTTA AMP MYSELF UP AS WELL AS YOU"

– ALICIA KEYS

THE SENTENCE

I'm before the period

on period

after the period.

I wont' sentence you to 20 yrs

but still sing songs in a minor

till they set us free

from these black and white keys

till they set us free

till they set us free

i'll still write songs

for the minors
taking pleas
prosecutor impaired
integrity pleas, PIIP
pimping the girls
like harry and jeffrey

I'm before the period
on period
after the period.

I WONT' SENTENCE YOU TO LIFE
BUT STILL SING SONGS IN STRIFE
TILL THEY SET US FREE
FROM THESE BLACK AND WHITE KEYS

"So, yeah, so what? It took me like maybe two years and s***

But I'm feeling more prepared...and I'm feeling a "lil" more ready for the world"

- Alicia Keys

COOKIES N' CREAM

all i know is pain

she is my joy

she saves me

she protects me

when i'm ice cold

i taste the sprinkles

on my cookies n' cream

to taste the pain of my

black n white dreams

all I know is pain

he's ice cold

no cookies

no cream

coldest winter ever

but it wasn't as cold as it seems

"I COME TO YOU HUNGRY AND TIRED, YOU GIVE ME FOOD AND YOU LET ME SLEEP"

- DMX

ALWAYS HUNGRY

starving for words
starving for herbs
hungry for pain
hungry for joy
when i starve
i feel more

always hungry
ready for more
more love
more vibes
more dark
more light

my spirit
always hungry
for the word
these words
serving sentences
confined to pen

always hungry
ready for more
more love
more vibes
more dark
more light
but should I take a bite?

"I AM THE BREAD OF LIFE,
WHOEVER COMES TO ME
WILL NOT BE HUNGRY"

- JOHN 6:35 NWT

APPETITE CHANGES

not sure what i'm hungry for
what used to fill me up
doesnt anymore

not sure what i'm hungry for
strings, keys, or he

i'm satisfied with this involuntary
fast

i don't want to miss the bread
he has for me

did I miss any moments?

when my appetite changes
so does my love
 my pride w/
the lust of my eye

"ALL MY HOMIES GOT PROBLEMS AND WE SELF-MEDICATE, WHAT YOU DO TODAY?"

- FOUSHEE

C.B.D.

compensate my body
damage,
even the pills
couldn't manage
couldn't manage
couldn't manage

*WAIT IS THIS C.BD. OR T.H.C.?

"BUT IF YOUR ENEMY IS HUNGRY, FEED HIM; IF HE IS THIRSTY, GIVE HIM A DRINK"

- ROMANS 12:20 NWT

#

i keep my enemies
hydrated

smart water
intelligent moves
gotta keep my enemies cool

i keep my haters
hydrated

keys soul care
2 splashes on my face

the rose jerico
hydrates my soul

IF I'M BEING PLAYED
(ode to dmx)

what these words want
from a poet?
u gotta let me knowwwww
u gotta take controlllll

is it a verb
a noun
a person, place, or thing

maybe my emotions
when Jah had me floating

in alkaline water
with the highest PH
hydrating my faith

is it the love
the pain
the misery

how u want these words
to go down

if i'm being played
heaven come down
is you with me or what

i'm tryna go to heaven with a jet black
crown

what these pens want from my ink?
u always seem to bleed

is it the color, the rage,
the black instant ink
the story
the vibe
OR
the clarity of my mind

i need you to clarify

"ENEMIES, THEY WANT ME GONE, EXPECTING ME TO WRITE A LOVE SONG"

- CHILDREN OF ZEUS

NO MORE I.C.E

NO MORE ICE

watered down vibes

i'm on wave

and you can't deport me

back to eden

poets without borders

"WORK BETTER UNDER PRESSURE, WHEN I'M PUT TO THE TEST"

- MONEYBAGG YO

NO MORE ICE

watered down vibes

i'm on wave

and you can't deport me

back to eden

"EVEN MY DARKEST DAYS, I KEEP A SPOT FOR YOU"

- FOUSHEE

NO MORE ice crushed enemies

THE CHOSEN COLOR
ALL BLACK
JET BLACK
JET SKIS

FOUR ROSES

4 roses

in a black box

4 thorns

our love is unorthodox

"i keep it all bottled,
you show me how not to,
i like your honesty"

- foushee

part 4 (memory foam)

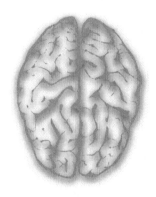

"...cause if this don't go the way it's supposed to go at least i'll know what feeling i'm going for"

– Liza

AFTER DARK

u know

mama said

don't play

after dark

the big payback

welcome to my park

don't touch the icy,

intoxAKating ivy

they call BRE

i know the game

better than quickley

shots fired in the dark

tickets to the park
higher than madison
square garden
no lower than melo
vibe Always mellow
i played off my anxiety
i Stay low like melo
underground track

baby don't play
man I love a tint fade

papa bear took me to
barber shop
daddy daughter co-op

just chill
sit still
bluetooth connect
black mans soundtrack

always 4th quarter
highlight reels
never show i how i feel
til u reveal

"THE ANGELS SAY TRUST
THE DETOX"

- GALLANT

DEAR BOURBON PT. 1

Dear bourbon

my love on ice
me and u
for the night
i love the way u hold me
the way u cuddle the ice

Dear bourbon

take me higher
hold me tighter

Dear bourbon

let's make love on ice

"I DON'T WANNA FEEL
LIKE THIS NO MORE,
I'VE BEEN ALL ALONE AND
VULNERABLE"

- LIZA

THE RYDE

come w/me
i'll find u
if u find me
our therapy

my thoughts
our beliefs
overflow
in too deep

ryde w/me
i"ll carry u
if u carry me
when it gets too deep

bre ashley

"i wanna ride with you,
i'm on a ride with you
i don't wanna wake
cause real life ain't
nothing like this"

- liza

R.U.F.F

life is ruff

my days are tough

but i have

R.EAL

U.NCONDITIONAL

F.AITH FOR MY

F.EAR

"MY MIND'S IN A
DARK PLACE
I GOT SHOT
BUT I GUESS I LEARNED
TO DODGE"

- JANINE

"i'm still counting
bullets
one by one by one
and i'll build a tower
for you
when i when i when i
when i am done"

- janine

BULLEITS

me and my bulleit

on the run

kentucky kinda love

no sippin til were done

rye lovers

aged under covers

me and my bulleit

on the run

kentucky kinda love

never leaves a trail

"EVERY DAY GETS DARKER, THE ROAD GETS LONGER. MY BODY GETS WEAKER, MY FAITH GETS STRONGER"

- DMX

MY MIND, MY SONG

i lost my mind [one time]
it was found in a song

i found my mind, [last time]
it was still confirmed lost

i hurt my mind [this time]
the lyrics came back refined
thoughts overlaid with cabernet

my mind, my song
will carry me home

trumpets
blow to my head

drums
wake up the dead

keys
keep me alive

play my song
to my mind
it believes its beliefs
get better with time
this classical mind of mine

my mind, my song
carry me home

trumpets
blow to my head

drums
wake up the dead

keys
keep me alive

my mind, my song
carry me home

[trumpets]
[drums]
[keys]
play for me
my melody

the cut
the color
the clarity

ONE time

last time

this time

one time

LAST time

this time

one time

last TIME

this time

BLACK B.I.R.D

Black

Inspirational

Raging

Diction

is this fiction
or a non fiction conviction?

I am the poet
I am the words
I am the lyrics

of the black bird

black ink
spills from from
my grandma's feathers in pink

hope stains the keys
of this lyrical melody
love pulls the strings
of this acoustic poetry

I am the poet

I am the words

I am the lyrics

of the black bird

justice screams
from the the strange
fruit eaten by the poe[tree]

maya and hughes
gave me a new hue
gorman gave me my cue

we are the poets

we are the words

we are the lyrics

of the black bird

"RIGHT NOW I FEEL LIKE A BIRD, CAGED WITHOUT A KEY"

- ALICIA KEYS

ALTITUDE

chosen

black wings

from the black bird

carried me home

i closed my eyes and

saw my frontal lobe

"EVERYONE COMES TO STARE AT ME WITH SO MUCH JOY AND REVELRY, THEY DON'T KNOW HOW I FEEL INSIDE"

- ALICIA KEYS

love on the brain
agape kind of pain

now I know
love is all I need

"THROUGH MY SMILE, I CRY, THEY DON'T KNOW WHAT THERE DOING TO ME, KEEPING ME FROM FLYING"

- ALICIA KEYS

now I know

my faith is all I need

"THAT'S WHY I SAY, I KNOW WHY THE CAGED BIRD SINGS"

– ALICIA KEYS

now I know
my faith is all I need

now I know
pretty dark elegance
pretty dark wisdom
pretty dark power
he chose my pretty black wings
pretty dark is me

"FREEDOM DOESN'T HANG FROM THE TREES"

- H.E.R.

POE-TREE

green garden sage burns

red apples on her tree

don't touch

don't eat

listen to this poe[tree]

this knowledge

this love

doesn't grow on trees

it grows inside of me

garden sage burns

apples on the tree

don't touch

don't eat

starve with me

here in Eden

i'll feed u knowledge

i'll feed u truth

FROM MY POE [TREE]

"DEVOTION IS MY NAME AND I GIVE MYSELF TO YOU"

- ALICIA KEYS

THE COLOR OF FOREVER

paint it for me
draw for it me
feel it for me

the color of forever

paint my pain
draw my devotion
feel my fate
draw my love

color it you
pantone kinda love
can you see its true hue

the color of you

the color of me

an artist's dream

the color of forever

PAINT my pain
draw my devotion

"TIME IS WHAT WE WANT BUT WE USE IT THE WORST"

– Niia

IN THIS ROOM

In this room
[he moves]

In my studio
I share my space with you

In this room
[he moves]

heaven came down
when he locked it down

In this room
[he moves]

in my studio
i share my space with you

MEMORY FOAM

memories foam
on her memory foam
pillow top only had
surface thoughts
countour pillows
fight back
lavender soiled thoughts
cost of consciousness

"MY MATTRESS IS black AND
MY back IS TOO"

- BRE ASHLEY

MY MATTRESS IS BLACK

my mattress is black
my back is too
black nerves s2 evade
check my discography

my spine is grey

my mattress is black
my back is too

the ink from L5
wrote the record for
the disc of L2

Dr.J said ...

Dr. J said I need my screws

so I became a black mermaid diving to
the bottom of the sea
for physical therapy ...

i dyed my hair black and watch the dye
float flat
as pretty dark waves
surrounded me
while the stripes of my swimsuit
healed me

Dr. J said

i could be anything

i wanted to be and

my black pain didn't define me

"DID HE THINK THIS S***
THROUGH?"

- BFF

LOVER'S BLOCK

Writers block is
More like lovers block

Maybe he is the poem
Maybe he is the words

There's a poem in him
My pen wants to meet

Last night he feel asleep
And I typed these words
To the melody of his heart beat

No more writers block
Just love on top
Keyboard swap
Til the music drops

Maybe he is the poem
Maybe he is the words

part 5 (tomorrow's sorrow)

"I'VE SEEN LAWYERS,
JUDGES, HUSTLERS IN
MY DREAMS
(ON MY WALK)

IT DON'T MEAN NOTHIN' IF
THEY AIN'T ON YOUR TEAM
(ON MY WALK)"

"...I've been takin'
backstreets just to
feed my soul
(on my walk)

You don't know me and
don't wanna see me
cold
(on my walk)"

-Raphael Saadiq

W.A.L.K.

Wisdom
Introspective
Loyalty
King

*my walk with the king

MY BACK

It's the L5 that keeps me alive

The teachers I had in 05

Awarded my vibe

They had my back

It's the blues that keeps me alive

UK blue is all she sees

Light therapy healed me

When the prism failed me

It's the YSL frames that
Hit all the angles of acumen
When I hated my brown eyes
They forced her to see bre

My back had my back

She held me down in surgery
No screws but still screwed up

Me and tiger are fusion legends
We already have the victory
Before I can see our injuries

In the woods we remain divine
We get better with time

It's the unwavering love
For my body
That saved me

It's the PRETTY PINK FAITH
Attached to my brace
We're strapped with hope
Armored with love
We got each other's back
To PT and back
It's the poems in my spine that
Carry me back to L4 (home)

"MY DREAMS ARE ABOUT BEING IN FEAR – AND BEING LOST AND NO ONE CAN FIND ME LOCKED MYSELF IN CLOSET"

– THE PAIN DIARY 2021

BLACK VESSELS

Travel with dark messages
to bring light to ur voyages
Near or far
I wonder where u are

These thoughts have travelled
To the remainderman
Of the captains estate
With Harriet in the lake
They wait in the water

In bottles that floated
We're messages from him to you
Stored in me

The black vessel
The black mermaids tail
Signaled to the sails

The Black Sea
Is never too deep
For a black vessel like me

HERE & NOW

Here and now

The vibe vows
The poet bows

Here and now

We allow
The comfort of how
The space of now

Here and now

Tonight
Love the light
My pen grip is tight

Here and now

Hold me tight
Don't say goodnight

I will allow

Here

Now

I will allow u
Here
Now

To feel my blues
Hear my soul

The fusion
Of me and u

Electric fuse
Voltaic muse

Here
Is the feeling

Now
Comes the healing

Let poetry ease in

Here and now
The vibes begin

PSOAS GAMES

Why are u so angry

I just woke up

I just gave u rest

We live in a constant state of spasm

I gave you ice

You gave me heat

Wheres my relief?

I gave you heat

Trust and believe!

Psoas hates me

I lost trust in him and me

*MAN PASS ME THE BIOFREEZE

SENSATIONS

Pain needs attention

Everything is a sensation

"YOU WON'T MARRY ME BUT YOU WON'T LET ME GO"

- Niia

CANDLELIGHT IN ME

Eucalyptus rain
Brings the flame
Clarity in the air
Optimism lives here

Rose with vanilla
Flickers over my Bible

"GOTTA SAVE MY, SAVE MYSELF"

- Niia

Scriptures sweet like

Mint julep

Garden sage

Calms the rage

"TAKE CARE OF MYSELF"

- Niia

There's a candle lit in me

Candle Light in me

Sun drenched the linen

I'm renewed again

"WALKIN' WITH MYSELF"

- NIIA

Oat milk

Spills on the white keys

Lights the black chords

Of my melody

"TALKIN' WITH MYSELF"

- NIIA

There's a candle lit in me

Candlelight in me

"STRATEGIC HOW I MOVE, I JUST TREAT IT LIKE CHESS"

- MONEYBAGG YO

part 6 (pretty girl gambit)

PRETTY DARK

i'm not that pretty

i'm pretty dark

into the night

i'm pretty lonely

if i'm so pretty,

then hold me

i'm not that pretty

i'm pretty dark

into the night

i'm pretty lonely

if i'm so pretty,

then hold me

if i'm so PRETTY, then hold me.

#

Don't leave me on read

Just to blame it me

Don't pour me anything red

Unless it's a Merlot

In a Bordeaux

Heavy pour

I'm a downpour

Don't hold me

Ur arms are too cold

For the warmth of my soul

Don't tell me to sip slow

I'm not urs anymore

Don't txt

Don't call

Don't catch me

Don't let me fall

"YOU KNOW I BE DOWN IF IT'S WITH YOU WHERE WE GOIN'? BABY, WHAT'S THE MOVE?"

– H.E.R.

PRETTY GIRL GAMBIT

What started as calculated moves
Evolved into the perfect groove

When my king moves I move too
When I slide he disapproves
Only hustle moves approved
For the queen's gambit

No stalemate with us
Just justified trust

Sans the lust
This some real love shit
we groove together
In law we trust
Chess can go on forever

gambit was hedged better then
Game stop funds
Investing and growing in this b****

We journal every day
He focus with H.E.R. on the brain

Same dreams
Same goals

Sorry not sorry
Call me Alexander McQueen
Couture for the queen
The truth is in couture
And the stories we publish
For the world

"MONEY WE MAKE IT
'FORE WE SEE IT, YOU
TAKE IT"

- MARVIN GAYE

v.i.p

I write my

very intense poetry in

v.i.p.

CLOUT: TO HAVE CLOUT IS
TO HAVE INFLUENCE OR
POWER. IN POPULAR
CULTURE, PEOPLE WITH
CLOUT ARE SEEN AS
POPULAR AND COOL.

- DICTIONARY.COM

C.C. CLOUT

i tell sissy watch out for clout,
separate inbox for our clout account

is this for you?
cc me
is this for me?
they don't even know
whose who
c1, c2

we were born into clout
it all started with doubt
nobody thought
we would make it out
CT Clout, ATL Clout
we quit popping bottles
dms got lighter

i tell sissy watch out for clout,
separate inbox
for our clout account

is this for you?
cc me
is this for me?
they don't even know
whose who
bcc me.

"THAT LITTLE GIRL WAS ME"

- KAMALA HARRIS

STILL SITTIN' PRETTY

pretty brown eyes
mint condition kinda pretty
no conditions on this beauty
exfoliate
with keys to my city
from neutrogena to
soul care
the love is still there

still sittin pretty
pink n green kinda pretty
saltwater pearls kinda beauty
s/o to the prosecutors still sittin pretty
lady justice kinda pretty
kamala kinda pretty

Sitting in the white house
michelle obama still sittin pretty
putting on for her city

my poetry sits pretty
chandon sipping pretty
pour a glass for my sissy
raise it up if you feel me

"CYNTOIA'S CURLS WERE TOO PERFECT FOR OUR IMPERFECT JUSTICE SYSTEM"

— BRE ASHLEY

INNOCENT CURLS

her
curls
bounce, play
while she pays a
permanent price

knowing kinks
are not a
crime,

yet, hair ties are
handcuffs
restraining our freedom
suppressing our fros

while flat irons pose

bail for the

low

P.G.P

it's a pretty dark vibe

Pretty Girl Poetress

darker than the rest

NOVEMBER REMEMBERS
(part 1)

I was chose to be black

I was born in the dark

I was chose to be black

I was born in the dark

november remembers

the beautiful blues I gave her

she chose these birth marks

one mark on my hand
where dark poems reside
one mark on my side
I chose to hide
how can my mark be so light?
when I was born in the dark

"CAUSE THINGS ARE HAPPENING THAT I CAN'T SEE, BUT IF I GOT PATIENCE, THEN I GOT PEACE"

-DJ KHALED & JUSTIN TIMBERLAKE

PRINCESS OF PEACE

glass slippers
dancing in her sleep
with her king
to the melody
of truth shining
bright her
black diamond ring

tears of gratitude
fall to the beat
of her defeat

glass slippers
dancing in her sleep
with her king
to the melody
Of truth shining
bright, her
black diamond ring

she is
the

princess of peace

bre ashley

"MOMMA SAID GOD TOOK HIS TIME WHEN HE MADE ME"

- LIL WAYNE

BIRTH MARKS

mark my birth
Birth marks
Chose sides
without permission

was I born in the night
did my birthmarks put up a fight
daddy was dark
momma was light

my light brown eyes
decide which side
left or right

pretty dark in the light
my birth marks shine bright

was I born in the light ?
did my birthmarks
put up a fight ?
daddy was dark
momma was light

birth marks
couldn't tell us apart

"YOU SAID I COULD ALWAYS SWIM SO FAR. I WAS LIKE A FISH IN WATER. SO WHY AM I DROWNING?"

- LAPSLEY

NOVEMBER REMEMBERS
(part 2)

every November
I get the blues of a sinner,
grief takes me under
I drown in my true color
pain takes me under
underwater
diving for my grandmother

WHAT IS DARKNESS?
(part 2)

it's a place i've been

    the aroma of when

        begins to linger

           the taste of lonely

           nights

       into the light

i see black

    i feel black

        i taste black

           chosen thoughts

                woven in as

                    darkness brought me

       into the light

bre ashley

WHAT DID YOU THINK OF PRETTY DARK?

First of all, thank you for purchasing this book "THE CHOSEN COLOR: pretty dark."

I know you could have picked any number of books to read, but you picked this book and for that I am extremely grateful.

I hope that it added at value and to your everyday life, especially the darker days, when you cannot see the light.

You are never alone and when you feel alone, open your eyes and see the light. If so, it would be really nice if you could share this book with your friends and family by posting to Instagram, Twitter, Facebook, and Goodreads. If you feel compelled, start your own book club or recommend this book to your book club.

If you enjoyed this book and found some benefit in reading this, I'd like to hear from you and hope that you could take some time to post a review on Amazon.

Your feedback and support will help me to greatly improve my writing craft for future projects and make this book even better.

I want you, the reader, to know that your review is very important. I wish you all the best in your future success!

AUTHOR'S NOTE

this collection of poems was written during the pandemic and ice storm during the coldest winter ever. few poems were inspired by the death of hip hop legends who have inspired me and made darkness feel normal, while others were late night thoughts fueled by intense creative vibes.

- BRE ASHLEY

ABOUT THE AUTHOR

she's astute, yet cultured. a humbled humanitarian. She trusts in couture, and verifies all vibes Brave, yet, adamant about rights. self-sacrificing, empathetic veins flow through her to her peers, colleagues, and the lost who she proclaims now found. indulging in details, analytics, logic assist her through highs, lows, and passionate dance with justice. mindful melodies fill her ears daily and soulful sounds pacifies corporal pain and renews the mind.

She is the author
She is the story
She is the creator
She is the designer
She is ...

bre ashley

Made in the USA
Columbia, SC
01 July 2021